Animals in the Mountains

A N I M A L S

in the
MOUNTAINS

RAINTREE PUBLISHERS
Milwaukee

This book has been reviewed
for accuracy by
Dr. Charles P. Milne, Jr.
Visiting Assistant Professor
Department of Biology
Marquette University, Milwaukee, Wisconsin

Copyright © 1988, Raintree Publishers Inc.

© 1986 Hachette, translated by Alison Taurel.

Library of Congress Number: 87-20688

1 2 3 4 5 6 7 8 9 0   93 92 91 90 89 88 87

Printed and bound in the United States of America.

Library of Congress Cataloging in Publication Data

Animaux de la montagne. English.
  Animals in the mountains.

  Translation of: Animaux de la montagne.
  Includes index.
  Summary: Focuses on sheep, goats, lions, birds,
and other animals that reside in the mountainous
regions of the world.
  1. Alpine fauna—Juvenile literature. [1. Alpine
animals] I. Raintree Publishers. II. Title.
QL113.A5413 1987 591.090'43 87-20688
ISBN 0-8172-3112-9 (lib. bdg.)

CONTENTS

THE BROWN TROUT

A BEAUTIFUL FISH

The brown trout is a fish commonly found in European rivers and lakes. An adult brown trout usually weighs between four and eight pounds. But some have been known to weigh more than thirty pounds! Brown trout were first brought to North America in the late 1800s. They are now a popular catch for North American fishermen, as are lake trout, a relative of the brown trout. Other types of trout found in North America include: rainbow and brook trout.

Like most fish, the brown trout's coloring matches its surroundings. This coloring helps protect the fish by making it difficult to see. Against the rocks and water plants of its home, a fish can be almost invisible. This is called protective coloration. The brown trout's color can be brown, dark green or even bluish gray, while its sides are lighter colored. Its belly is often a yellow or creamy white. The brown trout's back and sides are marked by small red and black spots. The spots have lighter rings around them.

Brown trout hatched in the wild are more colorful than those from fish hatcheries. Hatcheries are places where fish are raised. They are released later in streams and rivers for fishermen to catch. Trout grown in hatcheries also grow much faster than wild trout.

PURE WATERS

Trout need fresh water in order to survive and breed. The water must also contain plenty of oxygen. They grow quickly in cold streams and rivers with swift currents. Trout lay their eggs in water that is about 50 degrees Fahrenheit. But adult brown trout can adapt to water that is as warm as 80 degrees Fahrenheit.

Trout are carnivores, or meat eaters. They feed on worms, insects, small shellfish, and other, smaller fish. With its nose facing upstream, the trout hides in the current or behind a rock. It waits for the flowing water to bring it its food, or prey. Trout will sometimes even leap out of the water to catch flying insects.

SWIMMING UPSTREAM

Brown trout mate and spawn between October and February in northern waters. Instinct tells trout when it is time to spawn. They then swim to shallow water. Those that live in lakes or in the sea must swim up streams and rivers. Trout that are ready to spawn have two hard ridges on their undersides. The female trout hollows out three or four shallow holes in the river bed or in the shallows of a lake. Then she sheds her eggs into the holes. As soon as the eggs are shed, the male

The trout goes through many stages of development.

trout sheds a milky substance called "milt" over them. The milt contains thousands of sperm cells that will fertilize the eggs. The female brown trout may shed several thousand eggs.

The fertilized eggs hatch in about a month. In streams and rivers where the water temperature is colder or warmer, this time may vary. Trout will not spawn in polluted waters.

Like most fish eggs, trout eggs have a yolk. The growing trout feeds on the yolk while it develops, in its shell. After hatching, the young trout, called a fry, stays buried in the gravel for another few weeks. It feeds on the yolk, which is attached to its body in a pouch, or sac. As the yolk sac is used up, the young trout develops a mouth and begins to feed itself.

Young brown trout normally spend their first two or three years in the stream in which they were born. There they eat mostly insects.

As they grow, they swim downstream to the lakes and begin to eat fish. In parts of Europe and North America, the adult trout live in the sea until it is time to spawn.

A WARY FISH

The brown trout is a very wary fish. Like other trout, it has a wide angle of vision. This allows it to see almost completely around itself. Bright clothing, quick movements, and even footsteps on the ground nearby can all alert the trout to danger. A fisherman should move quietly along the edge of the river or lake where he plans to fish.

Brown trout raised in hatcheries make up most of the brown trout caught by North American fishermen today. Many of these brown trout are only a year or two old. However, a few trout always manage to avoid the fisherman's hook. These may live for ten years or more.

1) Trout face many dangers, including pollution, fishing and birds of prey.

2) Trout eat fish, insects, and frogs and toads.

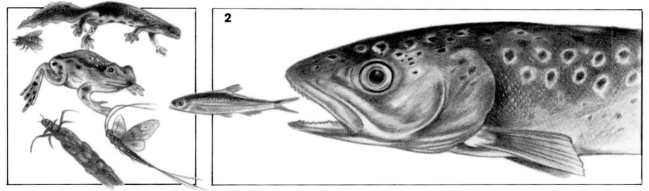

THE ALPINE CHOUGH

A MOUNTAIN FLYER

The alpine chough (pronounced *chŭf*) belongs to the bird family that includes ravens, crows, magpies and jays. Like ravens and crows, both male and female alpine choughs have entirely black feathers. Ravens and crows also have black feet and beaks. But the alpine chough has a yellow beak and red feet.

The alpine chough lives very high in the mountains of Europe. Its cousin, the chough, also lives in the mountains, but prefers lower altitudes. The chough has a longer, red beak and a longer tail. Both the chough and the alpine chough are about fifteen inches long. They are a bit smaller than a raven, but larger than a pigeon.

Alpine choughs live in large groups. They usually make their nests in hard-to-reach limestone cliffs and caves. Sometimes, however, they nest in buildings in the mountains. They can sometimes be seen perched on rocks and cliffs. They rarely perch in trees.

In spring, the female alpine chough lays from three to five speckled eggs in a nest made of twigs, roots and dried grass. The chicks hatch about eighteen days later. Young alpine choughs also have black feathers. But their beaks are black with yellow specks, and their feet are black. Their beaks and feet change color when they are about a year old. The young chicks are ready to leave the nest about a month after they hatch. Choughs may reach at least fifteen years of age.

A VARIED DIET

A flock of alpine choughs often gathers to eat in the same area. They carefully inspect the ground, stopping to peck at insects. As the group moves forward, the birds jostle each other. Each tries to reach the front of the hungry flock.

Like crows, jays and ravens, the alpine chough is not a picky eater. It eats many things. In summer, it finds its food in mountain pastures. It likes to eat insects, bird eggs, grain, and fruit. Alpine choughs are also fond of berries, such as blueberries and juniper berries. They are even said to visit the valleys in search of food. In summer they steal cherries from orchards. In fall they steal grapes from vineyards. Even so, they are popular birds in the mountains.

DEPENDING ON PEOPLE

When winter arrives, there is not enough food in the mountains for the alpine choughs to eat. They fly down from the mountains to visit towns and villages. During this time, they are easily observed. They often visit winter resorts in search of food. They perch on rooftops and sometimes land on crowded sidewalks or traffic-filled roads. Sometimes they let the tourists

In winter, alpine choughs visit towns and villages.

An alpine chough's egg.

The alpine chough's menu: 1) whortleberry, 2) cricket, 3) cherry, 4) grasshopper, 5) beetle, 6) bilberry, 7) worm, 8) juniper berry, 9) spider.

The chough is a cousin of the alpine chough, and also lives in the mountains.

feed them by hand. They pick through the garbage for things like old fruit and food scraps. When spring comes, they will return to their mountain homes.

HIGH FLYING ACROBATS

Both alpine choughs and choughs are famous for their air acrobatics. For this reason, they are a popular bird with bird-watchers. It is often hard for a beginning bird-watcher to follow these birds with binoculars. They move too swiftly.

They swoop boldly from ledge to ledge. They soar on the air currents, hardly beating their wings. Diving with their wings almost closed, they sometimes turn over on their backs in the air. The alpine chough is a more spectacular acrobat than its cousin, the chough.

Alpine choughs often fly in large groups. They rise swiftly through the air, skillfully riding the air currents. Then, when they have almost disappeared into the sky, the flock suddenly breaks up. One of the birds appears to fall straight down at a dizzying speed. One by one, the other birds leave the high-flying flock and follow. They fall almost a half mile before they regroup and glide off together.

Alpine choughs wait for hikers to leave so they can eat their leftovers.

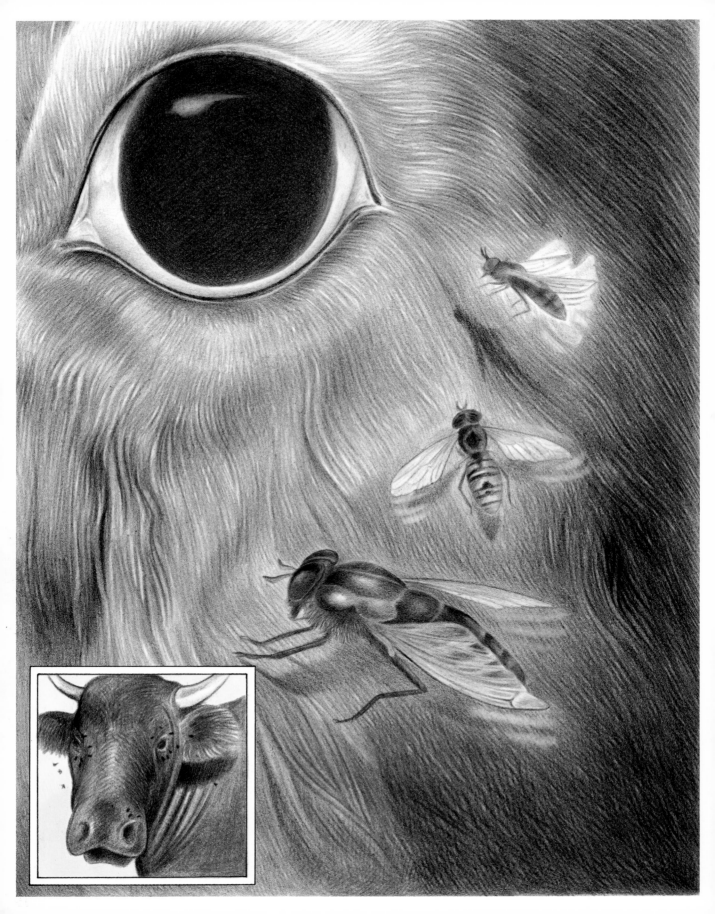

HORSEFLIES

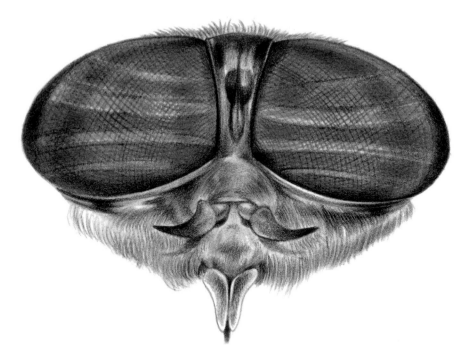

TWO LARGE EYES

Horseflies belong to the group of flying insects that include houseflies and mosquitos. They have two wings and large heads. There are thousands of different kinds of horseflies around the world. Some common names of horseflies found in North America include deer flies, horseflies, mule flies and greenheads.

Horseflies are medium-sized to large-sized flies. Their middle sections and abdomens are covered with tiny hairs. The largest horseflies can be almost an inch long. Their eyes are large, round, and often very colorful. The eyes of the male horsefly usually meet on the top of the head. The eyes of the female horsefly are separate. If you have ever been bitten by a horsefly, it was a female. Male horseflies are not biting insects. They eat mostly flower pollen and nectar. Most female horseflies also feed on pollen and nectar.

Horseflies have small pads on the bottoms of their feet, between their tiny claws. These pads allow them to climb on all kinds of surfaces, even very smooth ones. Horseflies sense heat, wetness, odors and tastes with their antennae and with special areas on their mouths and legs.

The female horsefly gives a very painful, round bite which bleeds. Horseflies can spread disease to people and other warm-blooded animals this way. In summer, animals such as cows, horses and deer may lose quite a bit of blood to hungry horseflies. The horsefly's bite can swell and hurt for several days.

LAYING EGGS

After mating with the male horsefly, the female lays up to several hundred tiny, narrow eggs. The eggs are usually dark brown or black and are packed closely together. Most often, they are attached to plants which grow in water or damp areas. Sometimes horseflies lay their eggs on rotting tree bark. When the eggs hatch a few days later, the larvae, or maggots, crawl out. The larvae look a bit like tiny worms with a pair of sharp pincers, or mandibles, at their mouths. The mandibles on the larvae of large horseflies are very sharp and can pierce human skin.

The larvae of most horseflies stay near water or damp soil. They feed on small worms, snails, tadpoles, and other insects. They even eat other horsefly larvae. After about a year, the larvae burrow into the soil to change their shape, or pupate. In a week or two, they return to the surface as adult horseflies. Adult horseflies usually mate soon after they emerge from the soil.

The first horseflies of the season usually appear in late spring or early summer. People and other warm-blooded animals must put up with these pesky flies until the weather cools again around the middle of fall. This is when the last of the adult horseflies die.

1) A horsefly   2) A housefly

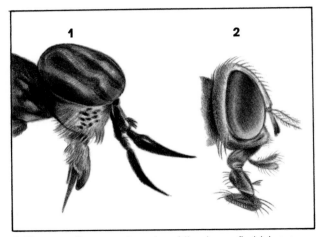

1) The mouth, or proboscis, of the horsefly hides a knife-like sting.
2) The housefly's mouth is a straw-like tube.

1) A male horsefly drinks some dew.
2) A horsefly larva under a leaf.

A DRINK FROM THE AIR

Male horseflies are not seen as often as females. They do not prey on people and other animals for food. They are known for two interesting habits, however. One is that they like to fly very high. The other is that they drink while they are flying. Swooping down at high speed, they strike the water's surface but do not stop. In a moment, they are on their way into the air again. This is probably a safer way to drink than standing still. If the flies landed near the water to drink, other insects, birds, and fish could catch them more easily.

TENDER SKIN

Horseflies usually bite where the skin is most tender. If you have walked in the woods when the deer flies were active, you may have noticed that they try again and again to land on your head and face. On a hot summer day, horses and cows are plagued by horseflies. The pests land around their eyes and ears, and on the tender skin on the insides of their legs.

Horseflies seem to be most active and bite most fiercely in hot, still weather. Such weather, often just before a storm, makes it easy for horseflies to fly. Because they breed near damp areas, horseflies are found most often near wet areas and woodlands.

Horseflies bother hikers near a stream.

You can catch horseflies with a butterfly net and study them.

BUNTINGS

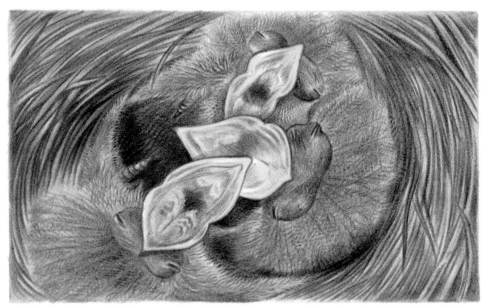

Buntings nest on or near the ground.

SEED EATING BIRDS

Buntings are small birds, about the size of large sparrows. There are many kinds of buntings all over the world. Buntings are also found in North America. These include the black and white lark bunting which lives on the prairies, and the beautiful blue indigo bunting, which prefers brushy pastures and the edges of woods. Like sparrows and canaries, buntings have short, strong beaks that they use to crack seeds. Buntings usually search for seeds on the ground. They also eat weed and grass seeds, grains, and insects.

In summer, male buntings are much more colorful than female buntings. In fall and winter, the male birds lose some of their colorful feathers. They then look more like the females. When winter comes to the mountains, some types of buntings travel, or migrate, to parts of southern Europe where the temperatures are warmer.

CAREFUL NESTERS

Buntings are careful nesters. They build their nests on the ground or close to it. Their small nests are usually made of twigs, straw and moss. They are lined with fine grass and hair and hidden in hedges or in tall grass. Female buntings lay from two to six eggs in the nest. The eggs are often spotted or scribbled looking. Only the female bunting sits on the eggs to hatch them. But when the chicks hatch, the male bunting helps feed them. The chicks are ready to leave the nest about two weeks after they hatch.

THE YELLOWHAMMER

In summer, the male yellowhammer's head and underparts turn lemon-yellow. It has dark streaks on its chest, and reddish brown feathers above its tail. When it flies, white feathers show on each side of its tail. Many people think that the song of the yellowhammer sounds like the bunting is singing "a little bit of bread and no cheese."

Yellowhammers can be found in low mountains, near open pastures and fields of grain. These buntings are fond of corn. They eat whatever is left in the fields after the crops are harvested. The yellowhammer's eggs are pinkish white. They have spots and dark scribbling marks on them. For this reason, the yellowhammer is sometimes called the scribbling lark.

THE CIRL BUNTING

Cirl buntings are a little smaller than yellowhammers. They have shorter, more rounded wings. The male cirl bunting has yellow underparts like the yellowhammer. But it also has a black throat and an olive green head. Like the yellowhammer, the cirl bunting also prefers to live in the warmer, lower areas of the hills and mountains.

Female cirl buntings usually lay two clutches of three or four grayish white eggs each year. The cirl bunting prefers to build its nest in the low branches of a bush rather than on the ground.

A male yellowhammer in summer.

The cirl bunting in fall.

Hunters catch ortolan buntings with nets.

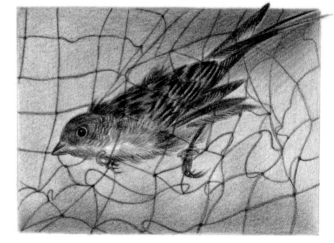

Buntings have short, strong beaks for crushing seeds.

THE ORTOLAN BUNTING

In summer, the male ortolan bunting has a pale yellow throat, and brownish pink underparts. Ortolan buntings also have pink beaks, and a white ring around each eye. They build their nests on the ground, often beneath the branches of a bush.

Ortolan buntings migrate from the mountains to warmer areas when winter comes. Before migrating, ortolan buntings eat very well. They store the energy they will need to make their long trip. Unfortunately fat ortolan buntings are considered a tasty treat by some people in Europe. Some of these little birds never complete their trip. Instead they are caught, cooked and eaten.

THE ROCK BUNTING

Rock buntings are usually found on rocky mountainsides. They like to perch in trees. The male rock bunting is easily spotted by his gray throat and head. It also has thin black stripes running along the top of its head and around its eyes. When it flicks its tail, white feathers can be seen. The female rock bunting is the only female bunting in Europe to have a gray throat. The rock bunting does not migrate. It simply moves to lower areas when winter comes.

A female rock bunting.

THE BROWN BEAR

A MOST IMPOSING ANIMAL

The brown bear is the largest of all bears. In North America the brown bear family also includes the grizzly bear and the Kodiak bear. There are few brown bears left in Europe. But some do remain in the Pyrenees Mountains in France, in Scandinavia and in eastern Europe. The largest brown bears are found in Alaska and in northeastern Russia. They can weigh as much as 1,500 pounds. When they stand on their hind legs, the largest of them may be nine feet tall. In Europe, brown bears usually weigh no more than 500 or 600 pounds.

Brown bears do not have to be brown. They can be black, tan, or even silver-gray. They walk with the entire bottom of the foot touching the ground, like humans do. They can run as fast as a horse for a short distance.

The brown bear has a wide, long head and a thick, hairy coat. It has short, round ears that hear only fairly well. But it does have a keen sense of smell. Bears also have short, muscular legs and big feet. Each foot ends in five stout, curving claws. These claws cannot be retracted, or drawn in, like a cat's claws. They are always out. Most bears also have short tails. A German folk tale says that this is because a fox once tricked the bear into using its tail to fish through a hole in the winter ice. The tail froze off, and to this day, bears have short tails.

NEWBORN CUBS

The female brown bear gives birth in the winter. She usually has from one to four cubs. They are born in a den lined with leaves, grass, moss and twigs. The den may be in a rotten tree, under a rock, or in a small cave. New cubs weigh only about a pound each, and are about the size of rats. They are blind when they are first born.

When the cubs are several months old, they follow their mother out of the den. One of the first lessons the mother bear teaches her cubs is to climb trees if danger is near. Wolves are a natural enemy of young brown bears. Sometimes the mother bear will even climb the tree after the cubs to chase them into higher branches. It is never safe to go near a bear in the wild. It is even more dangerous to go near a mother bear with cubs. Bear cubs stay with their mother for about two years.

Brown bears can live from twenty to thirty years in the wild. They live even longer than that in a zoo. Female brown bears begin to mate and have cubs when they are about three years old.

A BEAR OF LEGEND

Since the Stone Age, people have told stories about bears. In ancient Rome, rulers sometimes kept bears for pets in their palaces. And in areas of Europe where bears have been found, many towns have a picture of a bear in their village symbol, or coat of arms.

Newborn cubs usually weigh a pound or less.

In the Pyrenees Mountains, people sometimes set out food for hungry bears to eat. Then they can study the bears from a distance.

MOSTLY VEGETARIAN

Brown bears eat mostly plants and fruits. They dig up roots and eat buds and berries. Honey from wild beehives is a favorite food. The bear's long claws are handy tools for picking off beetles and other insects from upturned rocks. Brown bears also like to eat fish. They may catch and eat six or eight large salmon in a day if they are near a salmon stream. They eat the salmon meat and leave the bones and tail behind. Once in a while the brown bear may kill an animal as large as a moose or a reindeer for its meal.

Brown bears are generally peaceful animals. They avoid fights and usually run away from people. If they are surprised, however, they may sit or stand up and growl, swinging their front paws.

WINTER SLEEPERS

In late fall brown bears return to their dens. They spend the winter there half-asleep. Bears sometimes return to the same den every winter. Some animals, like chipmunks and marmots, hibernate in winter. Their body temperatures drop and they cannot wake up until spring. Bears, however, do not truly hibernate, and can be awakened from their sleep. Sometimes they can be seen walking grumpily through the forest, searching for food, in the middle of winter.

A zoo is a good place to see a brown bear.

THE DIPPER

WALKING UNDER WATER

Walking near the edge of a fast-flowing mountain stream, a hiker might be surprised to see a dipper leave its perch on a rock in the stream to feed itself. Disappearing under the surface of the water, this plump little bird actually walks on the bottom of the stream, completely underwater.

The dipper does this by facing upstream with its head down as it looks for food. The force of the water rushing against its back pushes the bird down. It then uses its claws to grip rocks on the bottom of the stream. As it walks along the bottom, the dipper searches for water insects and their young, or larvae. The dipper also eats small fish, tadpoles, worms and shellfish.

Dippers are usually found by fast-flowing clean water, and sometimes by the shores of mountain lakes. They prefer areas where there are shrubs along the shoreline. Male and female dippers look alike. But males are a little larger than females. They are about the size of starlings, and their wings are short and strong. The Eurasian dipper pictured here is found in Europe, northern Africa and Asia. Dippers have white chests and throats. Their heads and the backs of their necks are usually chocolate brown. Their bellies are dark brown also. They have scaly looking black feathers on their backs. The American dipper is a sooty gray color.

Perched on a rock, the dipper bobs and curtsies often as though it had hinges at the top of its legs. The dipper's short tail tilts upwards. Dippers fly quick and straight, just above the surface of the water. They often follow the course of the stream as they fly.

Dippers are song birds, like wrens. Although they swim, they do not have webbed feet, like ducks or geese. This makes them slow swimmers on the water's surface. When they dive, however, they push off with their strong legs and toes. They then use their wings to swim underwater, moving easily against the current. These birds are about seven inches long.

A DOMED NEST

Dippers usually build their nests near fast moving water, in hard to reach places. The nests are round, or domed, with an entrance in the side. They are often built on beams under bridges, or behind waterfalls. Sometimes the nests are built in the tangled roots of a tree at the stream's edge.

The male and female dipper work together to build their nest. It usually measures about a foot across, and is built of moss and grass. The nest is lined with dead leaves and feathers.

RAISING THEIR YOUNG

In early spring, the female dipper lays from four to six white eggs. The eggs hatch in about seventeen days. While the female sits on the nest, the male dipper brings her food. Both parents feed the chicks after they have

Dippers are found near swift water.

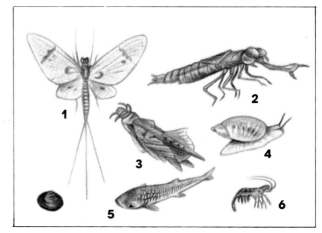

A dipper's diet: 1) mayfly, 2) dragonfly larva, 3) caddisfly larva, 4) snail, 5) small fish, 6) tiny shellfish.

The dipper sometimes builds its nest behind a waterfall.

Young dippers learn to dive before they learn to fly.

hatched. When a pair of dippers is nesting, they chase other dippers from their area, or territory. Dippers often raise two families, or broods, of chicks in a year.

The young dippers have gray feathers rather than brown. They are much whiter underneath than their parents. They leave the nest in about three weeks, but their parents continue to feed them for some time longer. Young dippers learn to fly when they are about three or four weeks old. They learn how to swim and dive under water even before this.

NO MIGRATION

Dippers do not migrate to warmer areas for the winter. They do, however, move to lower areas of the mountains where the streams are not frozen. The dippers need flowing water and are rarely seen far from it.

Because dippers spend so much time in the water, it is important that they groom, or preen, their very thick feathers with oil. The dipper gathers this oil from a special gland, called a preening gland, at the base of its tail. Preening keeps the feathers from becoming soggy when they are wet. The dipper's preening gland supplies about ten times as much oil as that of most other song birds.

THE MARMOT

A MOUNTAINEER

The marmot is a member of the rodent family. It lives in mountain pastures and valleys. It builds its tunnels on sunny slopes with a clear view of the area around it. In North America, a common type of marmot is the woodchuck. It is found in grassy meadows in the eastern United States and Canada. The type of marmot found in the mountains of Europe is called the alpine marmot.

Marmots feed mostly on flowering plants, berries, roots and grasses. After a big meal, they like to stretch out on sunny rock ledges. By the end of summer, the marmot is a pudgy, round creature. It has spent the warm summer days eating and gathering hay to line its den for winter. It may be so fat that its belly drags on the ground.

Marmots live together in large groups, or colonies. If you can get close to a group of marmots without being seen, you will see them visiting each other, playing, and pretending to fight by pushing each other with their paws.

The alpine marmot is usually a bit more than two feet long from nose to tail, and can weigh from six to seventeen pounds. Its fur is a yellowish tan, and its head is a light ash grey. It has small ears, and sharp, biting teeth called incisors. Long whiskers help it to steer its way through the dark tunnels of its underground home, or burrow. It climbs rocks and cliffs with ease, gripping the ridges with its claws.

HIBERNATING

Like many other rodents, marmots hibernate during the winter. The fat that they have put on during the summer will keep them alive while they sleep during the winter months. The marmots hibernate in their underground burrows. All the members of the marmot family help to line the large underground room, or den, with grass. When they are ready to hibernate in fall, the marmots enter their burrows and block the openings with hay, dirt and stones.

As many as fifteen marmots may hibernate together. They curl up into furry balls and tuck their noses between their hind legs. They sleep for six or eight months. While they hibernate, their heartbeats slow down from about 115 beats per minute to only three or four beats per minute. They breathe very slowly. Their body temperatures also drop, and can be as low as nearly 40 degrees Fahrenheit. It is cold in the burrow, but usually not freezing.

While they are hibernating, the marmots wake up about once a month to excrete wastes in a special part of the burrow. Then they go back to sleep. When spring comes, the marmots wake up and leave their burrows to look for mates. Sometimes they even have to tunnel through snow to reach the open air.

RAISING A FAMILY

Marmots mate only a few days after

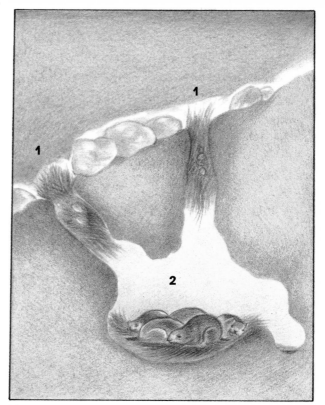

Marmots hibernate in large groups.
1) Entrances are sealed with grass, dirt and stones.
2) Grass-lined den.

The marmot cuts grass with his sharp incisors.

To watch a group of marmots without being noticed, you might need a periscope.

Marmots whistle and hide when danger approaches. Other animals, such as the chamois, hear the whistle and scatter too.

The entrance to the burrow is not very large.

Eagles, foxes and men all hunt the marmot.

they wake up from hibernating. About five weeks after mating, the female marmot gives birth to between two and seven blind, hairless babies. The babies are about as big as mice. If the mother has to leave them for a long period of time, she covers them with hay. Marmots raise one group of young, or litter, per year.

In three weeks, the baby marmots' eyes begin to open and their incisors start to grow. They begin to eat grass. When they are about six weeks old, they can finally leave the burrow with their mother. Before long, the young marmots are weaned from, or taken off of, their mother's milk. Now the young marmots eat grass, roots and berries like the adults. Young marmots live with their parents for more than a year. They are considered grown up by the age of two. Marmots can live between fifteen and eighteen years.

WARNINGS

Marmots have very sharp vision and hearing. When a marmot sees or hears danger, it whistles loudly. Then all the marmots in the colony run for their burrows and stay there until the danger has passed. Other animals, such as mountain goats, also listen for the marmot's warning whistle. They also run for cover when they hear it.

In the mountains, the eagle is the marmot's worst enemy. It often swoops down from the sky with little warning. Young marmots are also hunted by eagle owls and ravens. Foxes, men, wolves and bears all hunt marmots too.

THE GOLDEN EAGLE

LORD OF THE PEAKS

The golden eagle is a large member of a bird family which includes hawks, eagles, kites and some vultures. It is found in Europe, Asia, northern Africa and in most of North America. Because of its graceful flight, strength and skill as a hunter, the eagle has long been a symbol of freedom and power. The golden eagle in particular has always seemed to be the king of birds. In some places, it is even called the royal eagle. But not all eagles are so bold and strong. The golden eagle's North American cousin, the bald eagle, is not as graceful a bird. It is also more timid. The bald eagle lives by water and eats mostly fish or dead animals. The golden eagle prefers to hunt land animals.

It lives in the mountains and on the plains.

Years ago, there were more golden eagles than there are today. But for years, they were hunted heavily. Today, many countries have laws protecting eagles. Still, it is uncommon to see a golden eagle, even in the mountains.

The adult golden eagle has brown feathers, with golden flecks on its neck and the back of its head. Young golden eagles are also brown. But they have white feathers on the bottoms of their wings and also on their tails until they are about five years old. The golden eagle has sharp, curved claws, or talons, with which it grips its prey. Its beak is also curved and sharp, for tearing at its food. Its wings can spread more than six feet from tip to tip.

SEVERAL NESTS

Each pair of eagles claims its own area, or territory, for hunting. This territory may cover several square miles. The eagles build several nests, called aeries, in this territory. The aeries are built on high rock shelves, in holes in the mountain cliffs, or at the top of tall pines. They cannot be reached by other animals.

The nests are also used for raising young, for resting, and for storing food. They are made of branches and are lined with grasses, twigs and leaves. Over the years, the eagles add more and more twigs and branches to their nests. They can become quite large. Some have been measured at ten feet deep and five feet across.

The golden eagle's menu: 1) carrion, 2) young chamois, 3) hare, 4) ptarmigan, 5) marmot.

YOUNG EAGLES

Eagles mate, or pair, for life. The female lays two or three white eggs with red-brown markings in early spring. They are incubated for about six weeks. The male also occasionally sits on the eggs during this time. The chicks are covered with fluffy white down, and weigh only about three and a half ounces. The first chick to hatch usually kills the one that hatches later. So it is rare that two chicks survive.

Young golden eagles are ready to fly from the nest after about twelve weeks.

You can recognize some birds by their silhouettes.
1) eagle, 2) buzzard, 3) falcon, 4) sparrowhawk,
5) crow.

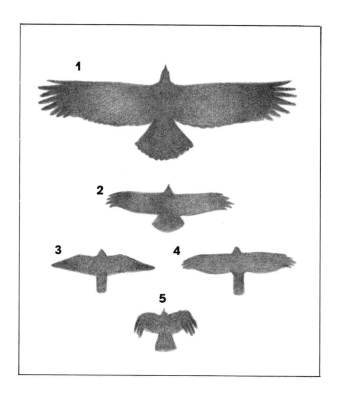

By this time they weigh nearly nine pounds. Young eagles spend their first winter with their parents.

A SKILLFUL HUNTER

Like other eagles, the golden eagle often feeds on carrion, the flesh of animals that are already dead. It is a skilled hunter, however, and also hunts marmots, hares, grouse and foxes. Golden eagles can even kill the young of chamois and small deer.

Leaving the aerie, the golden eagle rides the air currents upwards. It glides gracefully in large circles as it watches the ground below. The eagle's wings are constructed so that by moving just the tips, or primary feathers, the eagle can remain level and still, even in high winds. Like other hawks, eagles have very keen eyesight. They can see their prey, such as a hare or marmot, moving on the ground more than a mile below them.

Eagles kill with their feet and use their beaks for eating. Their feet are very powerful. Each foot has three toes pointing foward and one pointing backward. The toe that points backward is the strongest. It also has the longest talon. When the eagle clutches its prey with its feet, the talons pierce it like a knife.

Eagles often hunt in pairs. They fly low over open areas, looking for prey. When an eagle spots something, it dives straight down. It can reach speeds of about ninety-five miles per hour as it dives.

A golden eagle prepares to grasp an unsuspecting marmot with its powerful feet.

THE PTARMIGAN

A MOUNTAIN GROUSE

The ptarmigan is a type of grouse. Of all the birds that live on land, ptarmigans are found the furthest north. There are three types of ptarmigans: white-tailed ptarmigans, rock ptarmigans and willow ptarmigans. Rock and willow ptarmigans are both found in Europe, Asia and North America. The white-tailed ptarmigan lives only in the western mountains of North America. This is the only ptarmigan whose tail feathers stay white, even in winter.

If you met a ptarmigan high in the mountains of Europe, it would probably be a rock ptarmigan. In summer this bird lives on rocky slopes above the forest edge. In winter, it moves closer to the tree line in search of food. Like other types of grouse, ptarmigans live on the ground. They prefer to live in areas where the plants are no taller than themselves.

Ptarmigans are plump looking birds. They make clucking sounds like a hen, and also soft, low hoots. They eat leaves, flowers, berries, insects, buds and seeds. In winter they even eat the tips of spruce needles. Sometimes they must dig through the snow to reach their food. They get around mostly by walking and running. They can only fly a short distance. This is why they rely on their coloring for protection. If danger approaches, the ptarmigan stays completely still unless it is forced to fly.

AN INVISIBLE BIRD

Male ptarmigans molt, or shed their feathers and grow new ones, four times a year in order to look like their surroundings. Females molt three times a year. In summer, the ptarmigan's feathers on its back, wings and head turn brown, gray, rust and black. These colors make the ptarmigan look like the granite and quartz rocks in which it lives.

In fall, the ptarmigan starts to lose its brown feathers. The white ones begin to grow in. At this time, the ptarmigan prefers to stay in areas where there are patches of snow. There the ground matches its patchwork of white and dark feathers.

Finally in winter, the rock ptarmigan is almost completely white except for its black tail feathers and black beak. The male also has a black line running from its beak through its eye. Both males and females have a small red comb above each eye. The ptarmigan can make the red combs grow larger or smaller. It often does this when it is trying to attract a mate or frighten intruders away.

WINTER PROTECTION

The ptarmigan's winter coat of feathers is thicker than its summer coat. It also has feathers on its legs. In winter the ptarmigan grows extra feathers on its feet and toes to help it walk on top of the snow.

White-tailed ptarmigans change color several times a year.

1) in winter

2) in early spring

3) during mating season

4) in autumn

A ptarmigan egg.

The ptarmigan chick can soon leave the nest.

The ptarmigan has a short but rapid flight.

Ptarmigans often hide under the snow. They sometimes fly straight into a snowbank so that there are no footprints to show where they are hiding. There may be more than twelve ptarmigans hiding in the same snowbank.

WELL-HIDDEN CHICKS

In spring, the female ptarmigan makes her nest in a small hollow in the grass. Scattered rocks and shrubs also offer shelter on the steep slopes. She lays from six to ten eggs that are reddish brown and spotted. The female begins to sit on, or incubate, the eggs only after she has laid them all. This way the chicks hatch at about the same time. While she is incubating the eggs, the male usually sits nearby on a higher perch.

Sitting on the eggs, the ptarmigan is almost invisible. If someone comes near, she will stay with the eggs until she is almost stepped on. The female sits on the nest almost all day long.

The chicks hatch in about three and a half weeks. They leave the nest with their mother as soon as their feathers are dry. Often this is only a few hours after they hatch. If danger approaches or their nest is disturbed, the female ptarmigan calls out a warning. The young chicks scatter and hide. They crouch silently among the nearby plants and rocks. In their downy brown, white and black feathers, the chicks are almost impossible to find.

THE CHAMOIS

AN ELEGANT ANTELOPE

The chamois (pronounced sham'e) is an antelope that is found in Europe. It belongs to a group of animals called "goat antelopes" because they have features that resemble both goats and antelopes. The Rocky Mountain goat of North America is similar to the chamois. Chamois are skilled, graceful climbers. They are at home on steep, rocky slopes. Running from danger, they can easily leap a ravine that is twenty feet wide and leave an enemy behind. They can also swim if they have to. Chamois are usually active during the day and sleep at night. They may also rest during the middle of the day, especially during hot weather.

In summer, chamois eat mostly herbs, grasses and flowers. In winter, however, they eat moss, acorns, fruit, young pine shoots, small patches of grass, and plants called lichens. The lichens grow on rocks and tree trunks. During the winter months, chamois usually move to lower areas in search of food. Sometimes the snow is so deep that they cannot find food. When this happens, a healthy chamois can survive up to two weeks without eating.

In summer, chamois have short, smooth coats of brownish yellow. They are marked by white throat patches and pale bellies. Their faces are marked with dark stripes. Their winter coats are a dark blackish brown. The outer hairs of their winter coats are heavy and coarse. The inner hairs are very soft and fleecy.

Both male and female chamois have slender black horns growing from their foreheads. The horns are short, and grow straight out for about eight inches. The tips curve sharply back. Like other antelope, chamois keep their horns all year long. Male chamois can weigh from sixty-five to one hundred pounds. Females rarely weigh more than forty-five pounds. The chamois are less than three feet high at the shoulder.

HOOVES FOR CLIMBING

The chamois' feet are specially built for climbing. Each foot has two toes. The outer tips of the hoof are hard. The pads of the hoof are very soft and a bit elastic. These soft pads allow the chamois to keep his footing even on slippery rocks. The pads of the hoof curve slightly inward also. This means that the chamois can use the edges of its hoofs to cling to sharp, uneven rocks to keep its balance.

AVOIDING DANGER

Female and young chamois usually live in groups of fifteen to thirty animals. One or more chamois usually stand watch for predators. When danger approaches, the lookout stamps its feet and sounds a sharp, high-pitched whistle. Chamois also make hissing noises to warn of danger. Young chamois and females calling their young, or kids, make a goat-like bleating sound.

Hungry chamois sometimes visit farms to steal hay and grain.

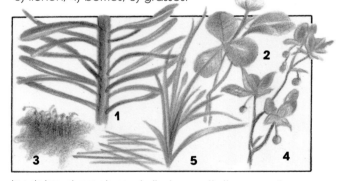

The chamois' diet: 1) pine needles, 2) clover, 3) lichen, 4) berries, 5) grasses.

In winter, chamois must dig beneath the snow to reach the grass.

A chamois looks warily down on trespassers in its rocky domain.

Eagles sometimes prey on chamois kids, and, more rarely, on sick or injured adult animals. Wolves, brown bears and lynxes all prey on chamois. Hunting chamois is a popular sport in the Alps. But it is very difficult to catch these animals. They are very agile and live in territory too difficult for others to travel.

SOLITARY MALES

Male chamois usually stay with their mothers' groups until they are two or three years old. At this age, they are considered adults. They then leave the herd and live alone in the mountains. The adult males join the herds again only in fall. Then it is time to mate. The kids are born about five or six months after the mating season, in May or June.

When it is time for the kids to be born, the mothers leave the groups and move to rocky, secluded areas. Females usually give birth to one kid. But they sometimes have twins, or even triplets. The kids can follow their mothers almost as soon as they are born. In their first few days, they quickly learn to leap, run, and keep their balance along narrow ledges.

If a mother chamois is killed, other chamois will take care of her kid. The females and their new kids return to their large groups in early summer. Chamois can live to around twenty-two years of age.

FACTS AT A GLANCE

Scientific classification is a method of identifying and organizing all living things. Using this method, scientists place plants and animals in groups according to similar characteristics. Characteristics are traits or qualities that make one organism different from another.

There are seven major breakdowns, or groups, to this method of classification. They include: kingdom, phylum, class, order, family, genus, and species. The kingdom is the largest group. It contains the most kinds of animals or plants. For example, all animals belong to the animal kingdom, Animalia. The species is the smallest of the groupings. Members of a species are alike in many ways. They are also different from all other living things in one or more ways.

THE BROWN TROUT

Phylum:	**Chordata** (vertebrates)
Class:	**Osteichthyes** (bony fishes)
Order:	**Salmoniformes**
Size:	7 to 11½ inches long
Reproduction:	Eggs are spawned in cold weather of fall or spring
Habitat:	Rivers, lakes and streams of Europe and North America
Diet:	Worms, insects, shellfish, small fish

HORSEFLIES

Phylum:	**Arthropoda** (joint-footed animals)
Class:	**Insecta** (insects)
Order:	**Diptera** (two-winged)
Size:	Up to an inch long
Reproduction:	1 to 250 eggs at a time; up to 1,000 a year. Four stage metamorphosis (egg, larva, pupa, adult)
Habitat:	Damp areas such as marshes, woodlands, etc. throughout the world
Diet:	Larva — plant, animal and other matter Adult — blood, water, plant juices

THE ALPINE CHOUGH

Phylum:	**Chordata** (vertebrates)
Class:	**Aves** (birds)
Order:	**Passeriformes** (perching birds)
Size:	15 inches long; wingspan of 29 inches
Reproduction:	One brood of 3 to 5 eggs per year
Habitat:	High mountains of southern Europe
Diet:	Plants, animals, food scraps, etc.

THE MARMOT

Phylum:	**Chordata** (vertebrates)
Class:	**Mammalia** (mammals)
Order:	**Rodentia** (gnawing animals)
Size:	23 inches long
Reproduction:	One litter of 2 to 4 young per year
Habitat:	Builds burrows in open areas of Europe, North America and Asia
Diet:	Flowering plants, berries, roots, grasses.

THE GOLDEN EAGLE

Phylum:	**Chordata** (vertebrates)
Class:	**Aves** (birds)
Order:	**Falconiformes** (daytime birds of prey)
Size:	30 to 35 inches long from bill to tip of tail; wingspan of 6 to 7 feet
Reproduction:	One brood of 1 to 2 eggs a year; usually only one chick survives
Habitat:	Mountains and forests throughout the world, except in Antarctica
Diet:	Small land animals

THE CHAMOIS

Phylum:	**Chordata** (vertebrates)
Class:	**Mammalia** (mammals)
Order:	**Artiodactyl** (even-toed hoofed animals)
Size:	3 to 5½ feet tall
Reproduction:	1 to 2 kids (young) per year
Habitat:	From forests to mountain grasslands of the Alps and Pyrenees in Europe.
Diet:	Grasses, shoots, mosses and other plants

THE BROWN BEAR

Phylum:	**Chordata** (vertebrates)
Class:	**Mammalia** (mammals)
Order:	**Carnivora** (flesh-eating)
Size:	5 to 9 feet long, depending on species
Reproduction:	1 to 4 cubs per year
Habitat:	Mountains and forests of northern hemisphere; primarily Europe, Asia and North America
Diet:	Primarily plants, roots, fruit, buds and berries. Sometimes fish and other animals

THE PTARMIGAN

Phylum:	**Chordata** (vertebrates)
Class:	**Aves** (birds)
Order:	**Galliformes** (fowl-like)
Size:	14 inches long
Reproduction:	6 to 10 eggs a year
Habitat:	Mountain slopes and open areas of northern hemisphere
Diet:	Leaves, flowers, berries, insects, seeds

BUNTINGS

Phylum:	**Chordata** (vertebrates)
Class:	**Aves** (birds)
Order:	**Passeriformes** (perching birds)
Size:	6 to 7 inches long
Reproduction:	Two or three broods of 2 to 6 eggs per year
Habitat:	Open areas, edge of forests, hills, and mountains. Found on most continents
Diet:	Seeds, weeds, grass, insects

THE DIPPER

Phylum:	**Chordata** (vertebrates)
Class:	**Aves** (birds)
Order:	**Passeriformes** (perching birds)
Size:	7 inches long; wingspan 12 inches
Reproduction:	One or two broods of 4 to 6 eggs per year
Habitat:	Fast-flowing streams or mountain lakes of Europe, North America, Asia
Diet:	Insects, small fish, tadpoles

GLOSSARY/INDEX

Aeries   the nest of a bird on a cliff, mountaintop, or other elevated location. (p. 36)

Brood   the young, as of a bird or insect, hatched or cared for at one time. (p. 29)

Hibernate   to spend the winter in a resting or inactive state in which body functions slow down. (pp. 25, 32)

Incisors   special cutting teeth often found in mammals. (p. 31)

Incubate   to sit on eggs to keep them warm so they will hatch. (pp. 36, 41)

Migrate   to move from one region or climate to another at specific times of the year, usually for mating or feeding. (pp. 21, 29)

Molt   to shed hair, feathers, shells, or other outer layers, often at specific times of the year. (p. 40)

Preening gland   an oil-producing gland found at the base of a bird's tail with which a bird smooths and waterproofs its feathers. (p. 29)

Prey   animals that are killed by other animals for food. (pp. 8, 37)

Protective coloration   a means of defense in which an animal's coloring helps it blend in with its surroundings so that it cannot easily be discovered by its enemies. (p. 7)

Spawn   to release large numbers of eggs into the water at one time. Fish, frogs, and toads all spawn. (p. 8)